HOMETOWN DINERS

YANKEE DINER. Route 4, Quechee, Vermont. 1946 WORCESTER.

HOMETOWN DINERS

Photographs and text by
Robert O. Williams

Foreword by Randolph Garbin,
Publisher, *Roadside* Magazine

HARRY N. ABRAMS, INC., PUBLISHERS

To my father, Robert Williams, who lifted me onto my first diner
stool back in 1961, and to my son, Gregory, whom I sit proudly
next to on Saturday mornings at the diner.

EDITOR: ROBERT MORTON
DESIGNER: ELLEN NYGAARD FORD

Library of Congress Cataloging–in–Publication Data

Williams, Robert O.
Hometown diners / photographs and text by Robert O. Williams ;
foreword by Randolph Garbin.
       p.   cm.
Includes index.
ISBN 0–8109–4155–4
1. Diners (Restaurants)—Northeastern States—Pictorial works.
2. Diners (Restaurants)—Northeastern States. I. Title.
TX945.W47 1999
647.9574—dc21   98–40698

Printed and bound in Hong Kong

 Harry N. Abrams, Inc.
100 Fifth Avenue
New York, N.Y. 10011
www.abramsbooks.com

Contents

FOREWORD: Hometown Diners

To better appreciate the challenge facing a photographer who seeks to document the classic American diner, please consider this little scenario:  Early one morning, an elderly man turns the key in the door of the small barber shop he's owned for the past forty years. As he has done every day since he first opened, he prepares his store and himself for yet another day of work cutting hair and shaving beards. He knows that he'll soon retire, leaving behind a lifetime of simple achievement. After all, he only cuts hair. He's never filed a patent for a great invention, run for office, or led an army into battle, but he performed good honest work that put food on the family table, and sent children through college. He kept his shop clean and well-maintained, while everything around it went into decline. Much of his equipment is old, and this embarrasses him a bit, but it still works because he's taken good care of it. The neighborhood isn't what it used to be, especially since the plant closed ten years ago, and most of his friends have either moved to the suburbs or retired to Florida. Soon he will join them. Then one day, the door opens and a young man with a camera walks in and asks to take his picture. "What on earth for?" the barber asks. The man replies, "I'm putting together a book on barber shops, and I love yours. It doesn't look like you've changed anything in thirty years." The barber finds himself extremely befuddled. "Is this guy kidding? This place is a dump!" he thinks to himself. "I haven't changed anything in forty years! If I only had the money, I'd have gotten rid of all this old crap years ago!" "They just opened a big new mall out near the highway," the barber says, trying to help. "There must be five hair stylists in there." "God, no," the photographer insists. "This shop is a treasure. It's exactly what I'm looking for." "A treasure? What's this guy been smoking?" This example may describe the bittersweet experience one faces searching for and photographing the quintessential hometown diner. Just replace the barber with a diner owner. Often, the story gets worse: our photographer takes the risk of being chased away by the owner wielding a sharp object; or, he returns a month later to find the diner demolished or blandly remodeled. It has taken a while, but the preservation community has finally come to accept the great American diner as a historical treasure. By 1998 seven examples were listed

in our National Register of Historic Places, and we now officially recognize diners as unique expressions of ingenuity and culture. People from around the world seek to patronize and photograph them. We see diner images everywhere, from television commercials for antacids to paintings in major museums. Restaurant industry executives and investors are pouring millions of dollars into the diner concept and have begun to morph the form into new upscale eateries.  Meanwhile, out on the back roads and Main Streets, an old stainless steel diner hums along under the glow of its neon sign. Inside, its owner and his help work the crowd, taking orders, pouring coffee, and sharing a story or two with a regular. The owner either doesn't know about, doesn't care, or simply doesn't understand why people are so preoccupied with diners. His concerns are more immediate: Will the refrigeration break down today? Will my help show up? Will the state impose a new regulation? The owner looks around and often sees an albatross. The building's too small, too old, and too far away from a major highway. He works too hard and makes too little money, but it's all he knows. In his first book on the topic, *American Diner*, Richard Gutman defined the diner simply as a "prefabricated structure with counter-service hauled out to a distant site." Looked at that way, we might well ask why anyone would need a book on the subject. Why the preoccupation with diners and not barber shops? First of all, Gutman's definition describes something uniquely American. In no other country will you find a similar enterprise—the prefabrication of complete restaurants for others to purchase and operate. But Americans not only love a good meal, they never seem to stop moving. Developed to serve both needs, the diner balances pleasurable necessity with efficiency, and coincidentally offers human contact, sociability, and a sense of community especially among travelers. In the diner setting, volumes of undocumented lore await the astute observer, whether they record with pen, microphone, or camera. Even as the diner eventually matured into the more formal roadside family restaurant, it still inspired stories, because despite the enlargement of menus, the putting down of square feet, and the addition of ornamentation, one feature remained constant in a diner: the counter. The importance of this fixture cannot be overestimated. As long as the diner retained its counter, the restaurant

welcomed the most loyal of its customers, the solitary patron, who because of the nearness across the counter of the waiting staff, the griddle cooks, and often the cashier, always feels among others, never alone. Atmosphere and operation aside, few other everyday buildings serving such basic needs express themselves so flamboyantly. Competition among diner builders has produced some striking architectural forms, all based on the transportation metaphor. These buildings did and do look as if they move. First, as lunch wagons, they actually did. Then as stationary buildings, the design evolved into an homage to railroad dining. With the launch of Sputnik, diner builders followed the rocket into the cosmos, offering a relatively short-lived period of space-age styling. But whichever form they follow, diners immediately convey the purpose they serve. Though we fill our history books with the deeds of great men and women, of presidents and generals, of brilliant inventions and bloody battles, most Americans have a more intimate relationship with lunch. At lunch in a diner, that relationship also embraces those who serve it. We may never know how the wisecracking grill man or the kind-hearted waitress affected the course of American history, but the individuals credited for those events have surely warmed a stool somewhere. Since one can walk into any diner at lunch time and find a composite of our national mind, no document of our achievements as a nation is complete without a close examination of where we eat. As it has for many of us, Bob Williams' relationship with the diner began in childhood. His recollections of sharing breakfast with his father are echoed by many who have also returned in adulthood with their own children to the stainless Mecca. While we typically prize our advancements, we sometimes feel the need to return to a base. Luckily for us, Bob not only returned with an appetite, and his own son, but with a camera as well. When I received a first phone call from Bob, I found myself more impressed by his credentials as a photographer for the *Philadelphia Inquirer* than his expressed wish to find diners to photograph. He wasn't exactly heading into virgin territory. Out of professional courtesy, I gave recommendations to him that would ultimately save him weeks on the road and moderate his cholesterol count. When the first results of our new collaboration came back, I understood the depth of his talent. Bob's ability to capture the definitive image inspires a wistful ache. I see the photograph and I want to be a part of that scene. I want to be friends with those people. I want that waitress to take my order. Like Pavlov's dog, Bob's photography rings a bell for me, and I want pie. These images by themselves justify the preservation of these roadside gems. One can make no stronger argument, because, in the end, diners are all about people, bringing them together, and making

them happy. On realizing that we have lost literally thousands of such places to what some have cynically described as progress, we only begin to grasp the scope of the tragedy. Progress, in my mind, does not value overzealous advancement of uncompromising efficiency over personal interaction. Progress does not strip our built environment of embellishment and human scale for the sake of saving a few dollars. Progress does not seek to extend our personal privacy into the public realm like astronauts into the void. And progress is not food petrifying under a heat lamp. ☕ True progress deepens our relationships with our fellow citizens, and progress expands our appreciation for esthetic expression. Progress preserves the one invention that manages to roll all this together, serving it hot and fresh with a steaming cup of coffee in a real china mug. And real progress serves it to a college president sitting next to our local barber, taking a well-deserved break after a busy morning at work. ☕ When you next find yourself sitting in a diner and you see someone outside taking pictures, don't duck behind a friend, display false modesty, or roll your eyes. By virtue of the fact that you chose to satisfy your hunger in this last bastion of humanity, you now play an important role in American history. Enjoy your meal.

Randolph Garbin
Worcester, Massachusetts

I INTRODUCTION

My fascination with diners began thirty-five years ago, when my Dad would take me for pancakes to the Empire Diner in Herkimer, New York. We always ate at the counter, because I loved to swivel on the stools. I've never forgotten those experiences. About five years ago they led me on a journey to document American diner life. I take photographs for a living, but these pictures grew out of a purely personal passion. The project has taken me from Maine to Florida in search of the living story of this truly American phenonemon, the diner. ☕ In order to understand why I've spent so much time documenting diner life, it's important to know how much I value family. For me, family is not a tidy little conventional package made up of a Mom, a Dad, two kids, and a dog. Family can be all kinds of combinations of parents, grandparents, uncles, aunts, and even just people who care about one another and a way of life. What does this have to do with diners? Let me go back a bit. ☕ I grew up in the small village of Ilion, New York, a factory town where virtually everyone had a direct tie to the main employer, Remington Arms, manufacturer of sporting firearms. The main street of Ilion had a movie house, a diner, several banks, a five and dime, two drugstores, one with a soda fountain, a hardware store, and a few clothing stores. In the early 1970s, Ilion's town fathers got swept up in urban renewal. They saw the three-story facades of the downtown buildings as old and out-dated, and they had a vision of a modern mall with plenty of parking. Over a three-year period, the main street was torn apart. Erected in its place was a shapeless box of a mini-mall with a dozen or so retail stores. As a thirteen-year-old, I saw my childhood haunts disappear and I knew something was drastically wrong. ☕ Two decades have passed and I'm still sad when I drive by the shell of the Capitol Theater, where I watched Saturday matinees as my father had done before me. The mini-mall is not a great success; the stone panels facing the outside are crumbling off, and the stores are often ignored by the townspeople who are now driving to other communities to shop. ☕ I can't bring my hometown back, but perhaps the view of traditional American life, family life, embodied in the diners I have photographed will inspire readers to pre-

serve those remnants of that other time. I feel a loss that my son will never walk to the corner store for an ice cream cone, or sit in the balcony of a movie theater to watch a double feature. He can at least still enjoy the delights of sitting at the counter of a diner, as I did with my Dad years ago, and he already knows the difference between that experience and standing in line at a McDonald's. I don't blame the big chain restaurants for taking advantage of business opportunities, but the limited menu and the sameness of food in them all is nothing like the variety and invention of diner fare. ☕ My delight in diners comes partly from knowing how they form a part of the American Dream, a dream delivered on a flatbed truck. That old lunch wagon pulled by a horse, simply got off the wheels and settled down. With a small down payment, a budding restaurateur could buy his dream, complete with pots, pans, and dishes. Working hard and employing local people, who formed part of the diner family—cooks, waitresses, dishwashers—he (or she) could build a new life. The informality of diners mirrors the democracy of America; they are places where a high-powered attorney on a trip can sit beside an auto mechanic on a lunch break and share talk about baseball or politics or kids, with the waitress passing by and contributing her two cents worth. ☕ My life has been enriched by diners. As I traveled for this book, I was rewarded with continuing looks into another time. And I had the conceited belief that my photographing diners would somehow enrich their history. It was the other way around. My eyes were opened wide to the fact that a genuine American way of life still exists, and the spirit exists in me as well. I believe that we must preserve these remnants of our recent past not as museum pieces but as integral threads in the rich fabric of American life.

PENNSYLVANIA

When I moved to Philadelphia in 1981 I had no idea that I was settling in a mecca of diners. Two of the country's greatest diners are located in Philadelphia, the Melrose and the Mayfair. Both share the legacy of having been family run since their beginnings more than fifty years ago, both sit in the heart of working-class neighborhoods, and both provide legendary meals. The Kubach family at the Melrose and the Mulholland family at the Mayfair carry on a friendly rivalry over who runs the best diner.

I was first introduced to the Melrose when I received a birthday cake that had come from their extraordinary bakery. It wasn't, however, until after a Phillies ball game at Veteran's Stadium on South Broad Street that I finally walked into this piece of history. (The diner is so well preserved that if you didn't look at a calendar you could swear it was 1956.)

Almost every night, the Melrose is still crowded after midnight; sometimes there's a waiting line. You may find that you have to share your table with another couple, and although tables at the Melrose have unique wooden dividers down the middle, they don't create much of a sense of privacy.

Every waitress at the Melrose is a seasoned professional who wears a pin with a clock face superimposed on a cup that shows the waitress's name and the year she began working at the Melrose. The waitresses have seen it all, so don't expect to try any smart stuff with them. They'll call you "Hon," if you're polite, but if you're rude they may show you the door. My advice is to treat a Melrose waitress like your favorite aunt, ask her how her day is going, and she might reward you with extra vanilla sauce on your apple pie.

The Melrose is the brainchild of Richard Kubach, Sr. who, when I last saw him at the age of eighty-nine, was still turning up at the diner every day. My son,

This is the second Melrose on the site: the first was moved to New Jersey, then was bought by the Smithsonian Institution as a piece of history. Unfortunately, through a series of blunders, the diner was destroyed. Certain pieces of history, just like animals, survive better in the real world than in a zoo.

MELROSE DINER. 15th Street and Snyder Avenue, Philadelphia. 1956. PARAMOUNT.

Gregory, and I had a chat with him as he ate a piece of pie on the back steps of the diner. He was cordial and warm, as I have found every lifetime diner man to be. Mr. Kubach's current Melrose (there was an earlier one on the site) opened on March 19, 1956. It is a custom Paramount diner with blazing red panels, and interior featuring murals of Philadelphia. Mr. Kubach's son, Dick, runs the mammoth business these days with the able help of a staff of more than 100 people, many of whom are forty-year veterans at the diner.

The Melrose Diner public area seems not substantially larger than most others, but the kitchen looks as if it is capable of feeding a small country. And behind this huge kitchen is a bakery that creates a wide variety of breads and pastries but also makes legendary birthday cakes that some people drive 300 miles to get. Both the kitchen and the bakery enable the diner to live up to the slogan "Everyone Who Knows Goes To The Melrose." But the Melrose is basically a neighborhood diner, and a real mark of the owner's concern for this is that the diner's garbage is refrigerated so that it never smells.

The Mayfair Diner serves the great northeast of Philadelphia, which is to Center City Philadelphia as Queens is to Manhattan. The Mayfair had an earlier incarnation as the Morrison and Struhm Diner, located at 41st and Chestnut. But the partners, Henry Struhm, Ed Mulholland, and Tom Morrison, decided in 1932 to gamble and move their O'Mahony diner to the then rural area known as Mayfair, which was designed as a kind of green belt residential neighborhood. I've seen aerial photographs from the period and Mayfair then was clearly in the sticks, but the owners had faith in the future of the neighborhood. They moved their twenty-stool diner, sprung for a new paint job, and renamed it The Mayfair. They also actively advertised the diner as a place to relax after a hard week's labor. The Great Depression was full blown at that time, but business was good, and by 1938 they were ready for a bigger diner. They went back to the O'Mahony diner manufacturing company for a larger model, this one with booths. The owners knew that the future would only be prosperous if their business catered to families.

A bit later, with the business still growing, they found a slightly larger parcel of land and moved the diner, adding a cinder block addition. Henry Struhm would again journey to O'Mahony in the early 1950s for a yet larger diner. This was to be the diner to end all diners. (Some say it was the diner to end the O'Mahony company.) Everything was custom, state of the art, truly a bridge between diners and restaurants. Struhm drove O'Mahony crazy by continually revising the design sketches and making as many as twenty-seven changes in the plans. The diner was delivered in the fall of 1954 but two years elapsed before Struhm was satisfied with all the small details. The cinder block addition was melded into this new diner in a custom renovation by O'Mahony builders.

(This historical excursion comes partly from my own talks with the diner's owners and longtime patrons, but also with grateful acknowledgment to Richard Gutman's fine book *The American Diner Then and Now,* which details the history of the Mayfair and many other notable diners.)

The Mayfair Diner today is the cornerstone of the Mayfair neighborhood. It is the landmark for geographical descriptions in the area and it is the reason why various small businesses still thrive in Mayfair. The man out front today is Jack Mulholland, nephew of Henry Struhm, and every bit the same perfectionist. Jack has chosen diner whites over a suit and tie, and this sets the tone for the working style of the diner: any job Jack asks of an employee is one that he's done himself. The diner gets a regular renovation every seven to ten years but makeovers are always a restoration of the original design. The menu also gets retooled on a regular basis but always remains true to its original spirit. The diner's cuisine is an outgrowth of family meals you'd feel comfortable with in your own home. In my view, the Mayfair sets the standard to which other diners aspire.

Melrose waitresses (left to right) Suzanne Crescenzo, Geri Spinelli, and Maria DeCicco relax during their shift change. Most diners have two or three waitresses at any one time; the Melrose may have as many as ten or twelve during the dinner rush. Most of the waitresses live in the neighborhood and stay twenty years or more.

OVERLEAF:
The Mayfair lights up the neighborhood at night.

MAYFAIR DINER.
Frankford Avenue, Philadelphia.
1957 O'MAHONY.

Cathie Gallagher has been a
welcoming figure at the counter
of the Mayfair for the last
twenty-one years.

SILK CITY DINER. Spring Garden Street, Philadelphia. 1957 SILK CITY

The diner used to be called the American, which I prefer to Silk City, the name of its manufacturer in Paterson, New Jersey, once a home of the silk trade. (An advertisement for these stainless steel beauties also once described the exteriors as smooth as silk.) I believe that diner names should reflect the towns they are in or the names of their owners. In addition to being misnamed, the diner also features a neon head of a Pontiac Indian, which came from a car dealership and is on loan from neon preservationist and historian Len Davidson. The Indian would at least make some sense here if the name of the diner reverted to American.

In the winter of 1997 I had the pleasure of combining my day job with my diner project. *The Philadelphia Inquirer* was looking for contributors to a Sunday magazine article called "The Region at Night." The object was to explore what goes on in the Philadelphia area after midnight and before sunrise. I proposed staking out the Silk City Diner on Spring Garden Street in Philadelphia, a unique spot with a lounge in a building attached to the diner that showcases starter bands and rising national music talent. The diner attracts people looking for food after the other clubs and the bars close at 2:00 A.M.

The crowd is an eclectic mix of the trendiest Philadelphia has to offer. The place hums with the chatter of patrons holding a few drinks under their belts. The waitresses have seen it all. I was struck by how they could size up a table before anyone placed an order. It took me a while to become a part of the place, but the atmosphere was hypnotic. As I sat there waiting for good photographs to emerge, I began to invent histories for the various groups of people.

I've since found other diners in other cities that function in a similar way: the Silver Top in Providence, Rhode Island, White Mana in Jersey City, New Jersey, and the Little Gem in Syracuse, New York, are all part of the brotherhood. The Silk City, however, is king of the world.

At the Silk City a lobby divides the club lounge and the diner. Junkies and the homeless sometimes enter there to warm themselves, buy a cup of coffee, and use the bathroom. The diner management takes a charitable attitude toward these people so long as they don't disturb the other patrons.

As the sizzle of the dance club fades down, around two in the morning, the diner awakens. The Pontiac Indian neon in the front window hums, beckoning the hungry aboard. And in they come, with their late-night uniforms of black on black, with just a piercing or tattoo peeking out to declare that the wearer is "On the edge." That is, until Monday, when they are back in front of a computer terminal at some center city brokerage firm or insurance company.

Most diner patrons operate in their own cosmos, but others readily interact with people nearby. Suffusing the atmosphere, the juke box plays an eclectic mix of Frank Sinatra oldies, Motown, classic rock, and up-to-the-minute groups such as Green Day. People fish for quarters to feed the machines and are taken in by the sign, which offers one selection for a quarter or four for a dollar: at two in the morning four plays seems like a deal. The food is great for late night fare and the coffee warms the soul, but every now and then you'll see someone order runny eggs and home fries and top it off with a slug of Maalox.

Diners aren't particularly known as pickup spots, but it's amusing to watch the interplay of young men and women who didn't find a partner on the dance floor and who give romance a second chance in the diner. One can also observe couples fighting over one thing or another, and young men flexing their muscles when someone stumbles against their table. Nothing gets too far out of hand at the Silk City, however, because the waitresses are all seasoned referees. If you go to the Silk City, go for the food, but enjoy the floor show.

Waitress Donna Etnoyer takes a catnap on the Silk City counter at 1:00 A.M. She had been on duty for twelve hours, and on this night her relief never showed up. Donna awoke to work another three hours. Donna treats everyone as she would like to be treated herself, but she also has a legendary temper. I once saw her react to a big party of customers who had spent an hour and a half monopolizing a table of hers and left a fifty-cent tip. Donna raced out into the night, winged the money at them, and let them know that they probably needed it a lot more than she did. All the customers who heard her screech through the open door applauded on her return.

Yvelissa Munoz and Angelo Zaccardo had been making the club scene in the Spring Garden section of Philly, an area that has become extremely active. Yvelissa and her friends seemed to get an energy boost at the diner and were ready to look for an after hours dance fix.

WAYNE JUNCTION DINER.
Wayne Avenue and Berkley
Street, Philadelphia.
1946 PARAMOUNT.

The Wayne Junction, covered
with graffiti, was closed
when I photographed it in a
summer downpour. It needed
a move to a new neighbor-
hood, because the once vital
industrial section in which it
stood looked like a ghost
town. The diner lost a little
of its dignity with each
wound inflicted by vandals.
Even its door, crafted from
stainless steel, had been
taken as a souvenir.

OAK LANE DINER.
Broad Street, Philadelphia.
1954 PARAMOUNT.

The Oak Lane was renovated in 1996 and 1997, and although the renovation must have cost a fortune and was done with the best intentions, the significant alteration in its appearance is, in my view, not for the better. This Paramount-built diner has some breathtaking wedding cake corners topped with mirror balls. A unique tradition persists at the Oak Lane: on each anniversary of the diner's founding the owners give their patrons a percentage discount off the bill that equals the number of years they have been in business. Last time I was there the discount was 45 percent and counting.

The wedding cake corner detail of a classic Paramount diner.

OPPOSITE:
Bob Wells, an old-timer at the Oak Lane, clowns with waitress Damita Wilson.

BOB'S DINER.
Ridge Avenue, Philadelphia, Pennsylvania.
1950 O'MAHONY.

Set on the plateau of the Manayunk wall, a notable geological feature of Philadelphia, Bob's Diner feels like home, although its surroundings—a cemetery— add a certain chill to the air. Roxborough is a neighborhood of Philadelphia, but I always think of it as a town on its own. Bob's is now owned by a guy named Jim. I wonder if there is a diner somewhere named Jim's owned by a guy named Bob.

Green Lane, the incredibly steep street called the Wall in the Annual Core States Bike Race, connects the bottom of the Manayunk hill with the top. This woman walks to the diner up Green Lane every day, then sits for hours smoking cigarettes and eating breakfast.

I never had the courage to ask this man his name. He sat reading the paper at the diner one morning, dressed in black as if he'd just come from a funeral, not surprising with a cemetery so close. In this neighborhood the residents will never be bothered by any noise from a diner.

The mingled smell of coffee and cigarettes, synonymous with diners since the dawn of time, will soon be a memory as nonsmoking rules take effect.

GATEWAY DINER.

Ridge Pike, West Norriton, Pennsylvania.
1949 FODERO.

The first time I laid eyes on Marilyn Huffard at the Gateway, I felt as if I had stepped into a diner of the past. With her pink uniform and perfectly coifed beehive hairdo she was frozen in time. A high school classmate of Marilyn's once saw this picture I had taken of her and remembered that her hair was just like that back in 1965. Marilyn also had a year-round California tan that added to the look.

I got to know Marilyn over my next several trips to the Gateway and I soon learned that she was a great deal more than a stereotypical diner waitress. The customers loved Marilyn because she knew them by name, remembered their birthdays and anniversaries, checked on them when they were sick, and shed real tears when one of them passed away. But as much of a people person as she was, she was even more possessed by a love of animals. She owned as many as seventeen dogs at one time, and not just mutts: she traveled the show circuit with prize-winning Toy Manchesters. She talked lovingly of their achievements as if they were her children.

In February, 1998, Marilyn died of a heart attack while feeding her prized dogs. It was a shock to me and all the customers at the Gateway. Just several weeks before this I was given a show of my diner photographs and Marilyn attended with her mom. I was delighted when she asked me for a copy of a photo I had made of her to send to her ninety-year-old grandmother in Arizona. The diner closed for the day on Wednesday, February 11, in honor of Marilyn, and the local paper ran an obituary on the front page heralding her achievements. Marilyn touched her community with gracious charm and warmth.

INGLESIDE DINER. Lincoln Highway, Thorndale, Pennsylvania. 1958 FODERO.

The Ingleside, with its pink neon sign, makes you feel like you're in Florida. You look for the ocean but see waves of shopping strip instead. What used to be country now hosts booming Philadelphia suburbs. Lincoln Highway still boasts fine diners, but, sadly, twice as many have disappeared. While I was working on this book, Earl and Edna Reese, longtime proprietors of the Ingleside, retired after many years of loving care for this diner and its customers.

I've been asked if this photo is a setup. To be honest, this is the way Hallan Usher, a frequent breakfast patron of the Ingleside, parked his 1955 Oldsmobile Starfire Convertible. The car and the diner are old friends and both are true classics.

SUNRISE DINER. Hazard Square, Jim Thorpe, Pennsylvania. 1949 O'MAHONY.

The sun fights the hilltops to peer into the deep valley that cradles the town. Ironically, the legendary American Indian Olympic athlete, Jim Thorpe, who gave his name to the place never set foot in it, but he is buried there.

CADILLAC DINER. Lancaster Avenue, Downingtown, Pennsylvania. Early 1960s SILK CITY.

Legend has it that this is the diner from the movie *The Blob*, but that is not, I repeat, not the case. The Downingtown Diner, which once sat on this site but was torn down, was featured heavily in the Steve McQueen flick. The Cadillac opened up as the Downingtown, which most people still call it, and it is probably the last Silk City diner ever built. Its huge plate glass windows and space age design are reason enough to love it. (P.S. If you are a real *Blob* cultist, go to see the beautiful Colonial Theater in Phoenixville, which was in the movie.)

KENNETT DINER. West State Street, Kennett Square, Pennsylvania. Diner type and date unknown.

In the narrow aisle behind the counter at the Kennett Diner, waitress Lynnette Albert leaps over her friend Karen Masha. Everyone shows a lot of hustle at the Kennett.

I resisted photographing the Kennett diner for several years since none of the original exterior remains and only about 40 percent of the interior is authentic. What led me back was learning of its history on the banks of the Delaware River, where the Chester Ferry has long been replaced by the Barry Bridge. The diner almost saw the wrecking ball before being moved to this sleepy little town, which lays claim to being the mushroom capital of the United States. I am glad I experienced this old gem in its new setting. It has a

new owner in Rhonda Knight-Mastronardo, who is only in her thirties but cooks like she's been at it for fifty. Her waitresses are young and full of spirit. The regulars are largely good old boys who discuss Chester County's bygone days and don't feel obliged to be politically correct. Over the years these same customers have brought in expired license plates related to eating. Among those hanging are EAT, ATE, 0-JUICE (from Maine, of all places), TUNA, CHILI, FRY, EAT-OUT, MEAT, PIE, BLT, and EGG.

DADDYPOP'S DINER.

York Road, Hatboro, Pennsylvania.
1949 MOUNTAIN VIEW.

Daddypop's Diner exudes the crazy charm of its owner, Ken Smith. Ken has had several careers and perhaps isn't done yet. He is what I would call a self-trained genius. How a man who designed helmets for the astronauts becomes a diner man I'll never know. A noted pack rat, he collects 20th-century pop culture, has two barber chairs at the curves of the counter, and antique toys and tools on every surface.

At Daddypop's all the regulars have their coffee mugs hanging on a rack behind the counter. Before the lights go on in the mornings at least a dozen people have made their way in the back door, poured their own coffee, and staked out claim to a favored spot at the counter. This circus used to be overseen by both Ken and his wife Beth. Sadly, Beth passed away several years ago but her spirit still pervades the diner. Beth's brother, Bob, runs the grill, and old-timer Mike Prue taunts the waitresses.

Ken Smith recently made diner history by buying the Tumble Inn in Claremont, New Hampshire, for his daughter, Debbie, thus becoming the owner of two diners that are farther apart than any in America. At either diner you may be given a pen that entitles you to a free meal at the other diner some 300 miles away. In my travels I have traded more than a few pens in both directions, and confess that I still have four or five of them in my glove box. Watch out, Ken.

Bob Strack, the most over qualified diner cook in America, balances work at Daddypop's, a computer repair business, selling real estate, and being an Amway rep, on four hours of sleep a night. He runs the day-to-day operations of the diner in addition to cooking. I call him Bob's Big Boy for his jovial nature.

Waitress Lisa Childs flirts with a perpetual fixture at Daddypop's, Mike Prue, who doubles as Santa Claus during the Christmas season, when he climbs on the diner roof to wave at cars passing by, then comes inside to take a Christmas wish list from each wide-eyed child eating breakfast at the counter.

JENNIE'S DINER.
Lincoln Highway,
Ronks, Pennsylvania.
1959 SILK CITY.

Jennie's, set on a slip of
land carved out of Amish
corn fields, has become
one of the last truck stop
diners in Pennsylvania
since the Birmingham
Grille went west. On any
given weekday its parking
lot gleams with the shine
of thirty big rigs. The
truckers share the diner
with a group of new cus-
tomers, the shoppers who
have just spent time at
the outlet malls down the
road in Lancaster. My son,
Gregory, has been coming
here since he could barely
walk. I'll always remember
the waitress who showed
Gregory how the wall box
worked by inserting a
quarter of her own and
playing her favorite tune,
"Bimbo." To my embarass-
ment, Gregory asks for
the Bimbo waitress each
time he returns.

Jennie's huge sign
says it all.

BIRMINGHAM GRILLE. Formerly at Route 202, Birmingham Township, Pennsylvania. 1951 KULLMAN.

This was a great diner that Pennsylvania lost. It now resides on the California–Nevada border in Truckee, California, lovingly restored in a town where tourism and skiers are king. I gave up the last two days of a seashore vacation to watch its departure, sitting in the stifling sun as workmen slowly secured the diner to a flatbed truck. When the diner finally rolled down the highway it passed the corner of Route 202 and Route 1, where it had spent its first twenty years of life. Shortly after that, however, the state police pulled the truck off into a highway department parking lot and fined the driver not only for having the wrong permits but also for having a load that was too wide by about eleven inches. The poor man had his wife and two children along for the ride to California, and several weeks passed before the diner finally left Pennsylvania.

THE NEW IDEAL DINER.
Route 40, Aberdeen, Maryland. 1952 O'MAHONY.

Four diners have occupied this site since 1931.
The New Ideal specializes in soft shell crabs and
Maryland crabcakes.

A view of the New Ideal from across the street
at a cemetery marker business.

Sherry Lomp touches
up her lipstick in the
rear of the diner.

HOLLYWOOD DINER

East Saratoga Street,
Baltimore, Maryland.
1952 MOUNTAIN VIEW.

The Hollywood Diner has had several incarnations but achieved national fame as the diner depicted in the coming-of-age movie *Diner*, directed by Barry Levinson, a native of Baltimore. Many people come to the Hollywood, which appeared in the film *Tin Men* as well, hoping to sit in the booth where Mickey Rourke argues with Kevin Bacon and Daniel Stern.

Barry Levinson loves diners. In his film *Avalon*, Levinson created perhaps the most loving tribute to a diner ever filmed. Through the eyes of a young boy looking in wonder out the back window of a car, we see for a brief moment a shiny new diner being lowered onto its foundation: fireworks explode in the background. This shot has next to nothing to do with the plot of the movie, but it says much about traditional American life.

Today the Hollywood Diner provides opportunity for disadvantaged inner city Baltimore youth. Run by the Chesapeake Center for Youth Development, the diner offers food service training and jobs as an alternative to the crime and drugs on the streets.

Eric Williams cleans the windows at the Hollywood.

DELAWARE

HOLLYWOOD DINER. North Dupont Highway, Dover, Delaware. 1950 O'MAHONY.

The Hollywood Diner in Dover, Delaware, has no connection with the one in Baltimore. Its location on the Dupont Highway, which runs the length of the state, once saw considerable traffic, but bypass roads around the capital city have slowed things down.

The Usual Suspects hang out at Jude's Diner.

JUDE'S DINER.
East Main Street, Newark, Delaware.
1953 O'MAHONY.

Newark, Delaware, pronounced new-ark, home of the state university, boasts a diner on the main drag among bookstores, pizza shops, and clubs. When I took my photographs it was known as Jude's, but for years it had been Jimmy's, and today is simply the Newark Diner. The owner at the time I hung out there was Jude McDonald, a real fireball. I spent part of a diner convention riding along with Jude in a bus and listening to her unreserved enthusiasm for diner life. An innovative chef, she had created a menu that offered the standard fare as well as an eclectic mix of vegetarian dishes to please the college kids who called Jude's home.

The diner had two lives; one, as a family retreat for Sunday brunch, the other as a late night coffee house for the club crowd from down the street. I lost touch with Jude as I ventured along on my project, and I came back to find that the sign had changed. The new owners were from Turkey and weren't sure where Jude had gone. They were equally proud of the diner, having replaced the Formica of the countertops with a new shiny layer. I wonder where Jude has gone: she was diner family.

NEW JERSEY

Comedian George Carlin once observed that there is a tollbooth every thirty yards in New Jersey. He might also have noticed a diner every mile, and maybe that's not surprising because diners are still built in New Jersey at Kullman Industries and Paramount just as they were forty years ago. For whatever reason, the state seems filled with stainless steel diners that never seem to close. They cater to the traveler as much as the local patron, and many are proudly owned by immigrants who embrace their new land by cooking some of the finest food on earth. Their names include Short Stop, Miss America, White Mana, Excellent, Tick Tock, and Roadside Diner.

Despite the proliferation of diners in New Jersey, many of my visits to them have involved long drives and crumpled old maps. I have done a good deal of cursing trying to get to these places, but the rewards have been fruitful and interesting. In the middle of one night I set up my tripod in the neon glow outside the Harris Diner only to have a waitress implore me to come inside before someone killed me for my camera equipment. I've had the surreal experience of munching a White Mana burger at 3 A.M. in Jersey City among a crowd that included a group who just closed the bar across the street, several prostitutes who were comparing notes, a couple of cops on break, and an opera-singing bread man.

Not all Jersey diners are such classics, however. Some will think of those huge diners with three hundred seats, a ten-page menu, and a parking lot as big as a ball field. For me, they don't embrace the true diner spirit; they're more like conventional restaurants, even though they are located at roadside. In them, you can't yell down the counter to a neighbor because he's probably at a table in the Crystal Room. My take on what makes a Hometown Diner would exclude any diner that could seat that whole hometown. Every diner in New Jersey has led me to another diner and another story. Those New Jersey superhighways, toll booths, and bridges are just the price of admission.

BENDIX DINER.
Route 17 at Route 46,
Hasbrouck Heights, New Jersey.
1950s MASTER.

The Bendix seems as much like a movie set as it is a place to eat. It has been photographed so many times that I thought twice about including it. But I couldn't resist because it has a great Art Deco neon sign on its roof, and out front there is a constant puddle of water that reflects the whole diner. The puddle's rut was created by the tractor trailers that often fill the triangle-shaped lot the diner sits on. My aim in coming here was to photograph the diner with sunset lighting the sky behind it. I showed up an hour before dusk, with every camera, lens, and accessory I could put my hands on. There was no excuse not to get a great picture. The day was glorious, with huge billowing clouds, the trusty reflective parking lot puddle was full of water.

As the sun was going down, I realized that the neon wasn't yet on, but I reckoned that they probably would be turning it on soon. I went inside, had a cup of coffee, and chatted with the cashier. I asked about the neon and was told that it was on a timer. The cashier clearly didn't understand my sense of urgency, so I asked for the manager and was informed that he'd be back within the hour. Now I was getting anxious, so I tried to talk the cashier, the waitress, and the cook into trying to turn the neon on manually. They all thought I was nuts. I thought about going into the kitchen and doing it myself, but as the sun began to set and my window of time was evaporating, the owner's son finally arrived. I explained my situation to him, but he said what I already knew — the sign would come on around seven, about an hour after dark. At that moment I realized that I had been pleading my case fruitlessly, so I hustled outside and took this picture in the closing light of the day.

BOUND BROOK DINER.
East Main Street,
Bound Brook, New Jersey.
1948 FODERO.

Bound Brook seems like a town stuck in the late 1950s. I felt as if I were in an old *Twilight Zone* episode. Freight trains rattle by on the elevated track behind the diner.

HARRIS DINER. Park and Washington Streets, East Orange, New Jersey. 1952 O'MAHONY.

The Harris Diner parking lot is swept regularly, the windows are often cleaned, and the approaches are decorated with carefully tended bushes and flowers. The diner sits not far from some seriously bad neighborhoods in Newark, New Jersey, but it is maintained immaculately. Bill Nicholas, a co-owner of the Harris, always dresses in white, working like a man possessed but forever looking crisp and dapper.

This cheerful little woman walked past my camera, smiled, and revealed a youthful spirit trapped in an aging body. She was out for her weekly visit to the diner with her nurse/companion.

OVERLEAF:
SUMMIT DINER.
Summit Avenue and Union Place,
Summit, New Jersey.
1938 O'MAHONY

The diner sits across from the train station in downtown Summit, New Jersey, a New York City commuter's haven from the hustle and bustle.

WHITE MANNA DINER.
River Street and Passaic Street,
Hackensack, New Jersey.
Late 1930s PARAMOUNT.

WHITE MANA. Tonnele Avenue, Jersey City , New Jersey. 1939 KULLMAN.

Considerable controversy stirs over whether the burgers are better at the White Mana or the White Manna. I have no intention of entering this fray. Suffice it to say that both are small, dinette-sized operations that serve little more than burgers, but oh, what burgers! These are not mass-produced quarter-pounders, but little bits of heaven that are best consumed in threes. Both Mana and Manna grill them before your eyes at round counters that showcase the grill man. Both diners were started by Louis Bridges and in their heyday in the 1940s they were parts of a mini-chain of five. Peter Genovese, in his book on Jersey diners, devotes a whole chapter to these two.

The White Mana was built for the 1939 New York World's Fair at Flushing Meadows and was moved to Jersey City afterwards, ending up on what is now the busiest stretch of road I've ever seen. If you want to turn around, forget about it; an accident happens about once an hour. Owner Mario Costas, who worked his way up from being a clean-up man to ownership in 1979 at the age of twenty-three, nearly sold the diner to the Dunkin Donuts chain in 1997. But when he found that they were only interested in the land and would have destroyed his pride and joy, he spent a huge amount of time and money cancelling the sale to preserve this landmark.

In Hackensack, a few miles north of Jersey City, the White Manna is smaller, somewhat better looking, and offers easier parking. Owner Ronnie Cohen is often at the grill, where delicious little squares of beef sizzle beside a mound of savory diced onions. It's the kind of place where people come in for a bag of twenty burgers at a time, where kids wolf down four at once to the horror of their mothers and the pride of their fathers.

THE SHORT STOP DINER.
Franklin Street, Bloomfield, New Jersey.
1953 KULLMAN/MANNO.

This dinette-sized diner has
a deserved reputation for
superior burgers.

TICK TOCK DINER.
Route 3, Clifton, New Jersey.
1992 KULLMAN.

This is a shiny new diner building, but it retains the
sign from the original Tick Tock. I love the expression
EAT HEAVY. It conjures up a vision of huge platters of
turkey and mashed potatoes swimming in gravy, with
a basket of fresh rolls dripping with butter.

ORANGE CIRCLE DINER.

Jefferson and Main Streets,
Orange, New Jersey.
1957 MANNO.

If it weren't for a local cop I met at the Harris Diner I would have missed this diner on its last day in New Jersey. It already had been divided into two sections by the time I arrived, and the team of movers was working to set it on the flatbed truck.

Several remarkable moments took place on this day. First, it seemed that everyone in the neighborhood came by to pay their respects, as if this was the funeral of a local dignitary. I swear that I even saw a few old women make the sign of the cross as they passed by with their shopping carts. Second, this diner was on a small corner lot with only narrow side streets for the big rigs to approach on. The drivers took the art of the three-point-turn to new levels: they edged past parked cars with less than an inch to spare. Third, the work crew hired to raise the diner onto the flatbed truck was from Central America. They must have been pyramid builders in past lives, because they rolled the diner from the foundation to the truck, literally inch by inch, using huge pry bars.

This three-ring circus offered several moments of personal discovery. As I climbed up into the diner for a look around I saw a thirty-year collection of chewing gum affixed under the counter. Later, as I peered down into the open canyon of what had been the diner's basement I spotted stacks of green-band Buffalo China, that distinctive dinnerware made in Buffalo, New York, and a staple fixture of diners everywhere. I climbed down into ten inches of slimy water to retrieve a dozen plates for my collection.

This particular diner's move reflects a kind of circular poetry. It was on its way to West Palm Beach, Florida, to a place where the Orange Circle could bask in the sun near real orange trees as it served a new family of patrons.

CHAPPY'S DINER. East Railroad Avenue, Paterson, New Jersey. 1954 SILK CITY.

Tucked away among the warehouses of a large food distribution center, Chappy's shares the neighborhood with two other diners, the Egg Platter and the Nicholas. It does an enormous take-out business, sending out an endless flow of those familiar blue and white cups of coffee with the Acropolis logo.

ROADSIDE DINER
Route 35, Wall, New Jersey.
1950 SILK CITY

The red interior of the Roadside casts a surreal glow on its evening patrons.

The Roadside Diner seems almost to be an art director's dream of primary colors of red and yellow. The singer Jon Bon Jovi, a native son of New Jersey, filmed a video here. But the Roadside's physical beauty has a dark side. The first time I journeyed there, in the pouring rain, I witnessed a heated argument between a waitress and her daughter. I gathered that they were living essentially out of their car, and needed the tip money from each day just to survive. The customers were the types that turned their heads as you raised the camera, even though you weren't photographing in their direction. The photo below, taken a year later shows, if you look closely, that the diner has been wrapped in police tape. My first thought was, who was murdered and why, but it turned out that a small kitchen fire had led to health code citations and a temporary closure. I hope that it has risen from the ashes and shines again, as it does in this sunset.

CLUB DINER. Black Horse Pike, Bellmawr, New Jersey. 1963 KULLMAN.

The Kullman Company had been building diners for
thirty years by the time they created this 1963 space
station. When other diner manufacturers folded in the
early 1960s, Kullman broke new ground with amazing
diners with wide-pane glass windows.

BURLINGTON DINER. Route 130 and High Street, Burlington, New Jersey. 1950s DeRAFFELLE.

If you want to know if the owner is in attendance, just look for his Cadillac parked on the sidewalk out front. Clearly, when I took this picture he wasn't there.

ANGIE'S BRIDGETON GRILL. East Broad Street, Bridgeton, New Jersey, 1940 SILK CITY.

It is said that the key to good real estate is location, location, location. Angie's literally sits on the bridge into town, on a lot only inches bigger than the diner itself. Angie Perry, an ageless veteran, still cooks the soups.

SALEM OAK DINER.   West Broadway and Oak Street, Salem, New Jersey. 1954 SILK CITY.

Owner Bob McAllister's father, also named Bob McAllister, bought this diner with winnings from a big day at the track. The wise winner invested his dough in the stainless steel gem that sits opposite a historic cemetery across the street that is shaded by the five-hundred-year-old Charter Oak tree. Bob, Jr. courted his wife, Barbara, in the back booths of the diner, and later became the master chef of the Salem Oak, with Barbara out front at the register, and all his children either cooking or waiting tables.

ABOVE: Waitresses share in decorations for July 4.

Gianna Montanez, age 3, prepares to play a song on the wall box.

The Elgin Diner sits on the outskirts of Camden on a street that was filled with shops and markets thirty years ago and has been derelict for some time. Camden needs a helping hand, and the Elgin delivers that in many ways.

James C. Robinson, age 81, and better known as Dunky, smokes his trademark cigar at the Elgin counter at breakfast.

ELGIN DINER. Mount Ephraim Avenue, Camden, New Jersey. 1958 KULLMAN.

MUSTACHE BILL'S.
8th Street and Broadway,
Barnegat Light, New Jersey.
1959 FODERO.

At first glance this diner
seems out of place among
the vacation properties that
lace Long Beach Island. But
it's just what the doctor
ordered: I can't think of a
better treat than walking
along the beach from a
rented summer house to
Mustache Bill's. Above, father
and son share a Saturday
morning breakfast at Mus-
tache Bill's.

The bicycles in front make it
seem as if you're always on a
vacation when you eat at
Mustache Bill's.

WILDWOOD DINER.
Spencer and Atlantic Avenues,
Wildwood, New Jersey.
1958 SUPERIOR

I first knew this diner twenty years
ago, when I used to spend wild week-
ends in Wildwood. The town fits its
name each year when thousands of
high school kids converge here for a
traditional Pennsylvania–New Jersey
rite of passage, senior week. Wildwood offers a classic collection of
space-age style 1960s motels, with
garish neon signs. I hope that they are
never torn down, for this is a collection of authentic period architectural
treasures not unlike the main drag of
Las Vegas, and just as worthy as the
Victorian splendor of Cape May, five
miles down the coast. The Wildwood
Diner is a rare Superior-brand diner
of a vintage in keeping with the rest
of town. Its Mediterranean decor
interior is a little disappointing, but
the quality of the waitresses and the
food make up for it.

Some customers
get more than a plate
of toast with their
breakfast.

ANGELO'S. North Main Street, Glassboro, New Jersey. 1951 KULLMAN.

Tiffany's mom couldn't
find a babysitter, so she
brought her daughter to
work. Tiffany entertained
the customers and tor-
tured her mother. When I
arrived, the poor woman
had essentially worked a
double shift, one waiting
on customers and another
waiting on Tiffany.

HAMMONTON DINER. Railroad Avenue, Hammonton, New Jersey. 1946 KULLMAN.

CONNECTICUT

O'ROURKE'S DINER.
Main Street, Middletown, Connecticut.
1946 MOUNTAIN VIEW.

Brian O'Rourke is a legendary diner proprietor. In addition to running a first-class eating establishment, Brian operates a one-man charitable trust. A fellow once came into O'Rourke's in a total panic because his car had broken down and he was on the way to the job interview of a lifetime. He was devastated. Without blinking, Brian threw the man the keys to his own car and told him to go and get the job. He did, and O'Rourke's earned a new lifetime customer, one person at a time.

More than a Samaritan, Brian is the saint of soups. People come in for the soup of the day as if called by divine inspiration. Brian's soups are meals in themselves. He actually has a menu item called a Soup Sampler. To create his delicious liquid meals he uses the finest vegetables, fresh cream, wine that could easily be served by the glass, and chunks of chicken, beef, or fish. Brian's soups really qualify as stews.

Exterior of O'Rourke's at sunset.

OPPOSITE:
Gregory, the cook, takes a smoke outside the diner.

COLLIN'S DINER.
Railroad Square, North Canaan,
Connecticut.
1942 O'MAHONY.

This feast of blue sits at the
bottom of the hill near the
train station.

Gary Zemola bags a customer's order in the tight confines of the Weenie truck.

SUPER DUPER WEENIE TRUCK.
Black Rock Turnpike, Fairfield, Connecticut.

Gary Zemola is the Young Turk of the diner world, a unique personality who charms everyone he meets with his direct and honest approach. With his brush-cut haircut and gravel voice, Gary seems like a character from a Brooklyn buddies flick. He will be the number one diner man in America if he can get the diner that he owns up and running. It has been sitting on blocks in a salvage yard. For now, he operates from the tight constraints of the Super Duper Weenie, the finest lunch wagon in America.

Gary is a Cordon Bleu chef hiding in the apron of a hot dog vendor. He graduated from the Culinary Institute of America in Hyde Park, New York, probably America's premier training school for professional cooks, and he worked at a number of fine restaurants before he ended up with the lunch wagon. Like the character in the movie *Field of Dreams*, Gary had a vision. He was looking through John Baeder's book *Diners*, when he became fascinated by the Super Duper Weenie Truck pictured therein. He determined not only to find it, but to own it. Through persistence he was able to locate it, discovering that it was considerably beaten up. Nonetheless, he bought it, had the engine overhauled, and invested in a new paint job, using as a guide the details in Baeder's painting. Now the thirty-year-old truck is immaculate inside and out.

Gary tried several locations for his portable restaurant, but eventually ended up close to home. The wagon sits just off Exit 24 of Highway I-95, in the parking lot of his father's electrical supply business in Fairfield.

I visited Gary on a cold, overcast day one winter, and spent the lunch hour in the tight constraints of his truck. I got a firsthand taste of how he works and what he serves. Trust me, it's not all hot dogs, although his hot dogs, with their homemade relishes, are superior to anything you've tasted. Gary insisted that I try every item on his menu as he cooked, chatted with customers, and talked on the portable phone that seems to grow from his ear.

Gary's truck is a model of efficiency. At one end there are the deep fryers for the French fries, and burners to warm the soups that he prepares at home the night before. Every batch of French fries is freshly cut in a gizmo mounted on the counter. The potato strips jump in the oil seconds after being sliced. No fast food chain French fry should ever show its face on the same plate as Gary's. But the real triumph of the Weenie Man's menu is the soup. Each day Gary creates a bowl of heaven in his soups. They combine fresh ingredients with divine inspiration. I'd love to describe them all, but instead would rather suggest that you get in your car and just drive, not really knowing where you're going, but trusting that the *Field of Dreams* will guide you. ("If you build it, they will come.") Sooner or later, the car will cross into Connecticut. You'll arrive at Gary's truck feeling famished. You'll sample the best soup since your grandmother warmed your belly as a child. You'll vow to never eat soup from a can again.

After several years of running the Super Duper Weenie, Gary had the dream again: this time it told him that his time for a full-size diner had come. As in most negotiations there were several missteps, but in 1996 he bought Gina's Diner in Meriden, Connecticut. It is a 1941 Silk City (number 4173), with glorious blue tile inside. O. B. Hill, the nation's premier diner mover, transported Gary's dream to a salvage yard around the corner from the parking lot where his Super Duper Weenie Truck resides, and Gary began the monumental task of restoring his dream. He stripped off the old, rusted porcelain panels, finding decay in the wood frame and virtually no insulation. With guidance from Dan Zilka, a friend and diner restoration expert, Gary began repairing the wounds of years of neglect.

At this point I'd love to report that the diner is up and running. A major stumbling block is in Gary's way: he needs the land to build his dream on. Gary will never give up, but he has an uphill battle with real estate prices in Fairfield County. The beauty is that he's worked to achieve his dream, and when it reaches fruition it will never be taken for granted.

THE MODERN DINER. East Avenue, Pawtucket, Rhode Island. 1940 STERLING STREAMLINER.

The ultimate streamliner diner, the Modern, which serves a working-class neighborhood in Pawtucket, was the first diner to be placed on the National Historic Register.

SILVER TOP DINER. Harris Street, Providence, Rhode Island. 1941 KULLMAN.

One of the great group of late night eateries, the Silver Top is easy to see from the Interstate, but tough to get to once you make the decision to drive off the high-way. It sits in a bustling warehouse district and, until recently, had the unusual open hours of 11 P.M. to 7:00 A.M. It is clearly the place to be in Providence after the bars have closed and you crave eggs and toast to cure your hangover. It shares a kindred spirit with the Silk City Diner of Philadelphia, and is equally notable for its electric customers, who shine even after the lights have been turned off.

ABOVE:
The exterior of the Silver Top glows as the sun rises, and one of Providence's finest can be seen inside drinking coffee.

OVERLEAF:
Local college kids carry on at 4:00 in the morning, jumping from booth to booth at the Silver Top.

JIGGER'S DINER. Main Street, East Greenwich, Rhode Island. 1947 WORCESTER.

Carol Shriner behind the counter at Jigger's.

I used to think the name of this diner was Tiggers, like the Winnie the Pooh character, because of the script used in the logo. Before owner Carol Shriner got her hands on Jigger's it was used as a storeroom for paint by the adjacent hardware store. When Carol took over she had the monumental task of replacing the counter, fixtures, and too many appliances to name. One item, the diner's classic Worcester clock, returned home when the honest citizen who had "salvaged" the timepiece returned it to complete the restoration. When I first laid eyes on the diner I couldn't believe that what I was looking at wasn't all original.

When I first ate at Jigger's the place was packed and, sadly, they had run out of my favorite diner meal, roast turkey. I had the Yankee pot roast instead, and was equally pleased. Carol Shriner is the essence of grace under pressure. She isn't quite sure why people make such a fuss over her diner, but she's glad for the good business.

MASSACHUSETTS

If you die and go to diner heaven, you'll find that it's located in Massachusetts. Although New Jersey may have more diners, Massachusetts has the greatest collection. They have all the records for the oldest and the smallest, and some so rare you've never seen any like them before. After traveling up and down the East Coast, I realized that more than half of my favorites reside in Massachusetts.

In order to hunt diners correctly in Massachusetts you need to start in the middle of the state, in Worcester. Branching out from Worcester in any direction you can find diners running strong in a hundred different towns. The great ones are operated by folks willing to work eighty hours a week to make their diners the best places to eat in their towns.

We begin in Worcester, however, because the city was home to the biggest little diner manufacturer of all, the Worcester Lunch Car Company. The company started in 1906 and closed in 1961. They built 651 diners, mostly from wood, handcrafted little diners that bear little resemblance to their stainless steel cousins from New Jersey, and the firm passed into history when it couldn't keep up with the trend toward bigger, shinier diners.

Worcester has several living memorials to the manufacturer, including the Boulevard Diner, which is thought by many to be the prettiest diner anywhere. If you want some incredibly good food, think of Charlie's Diner and the Parkway, both in Worcester. To be honest, the first time I ever ate Italian food in a diner was in Worcester, which has a strong Italian-American community. When in Worcester do as the locals do.

In Worcester I also met one of the greatest advocates of diners in America, Randolph Garbin. Randy is publisher of *Roadside* magazine, a journal devoted to the pleasures of the road. Randy doesn't try to enshrine diners, he wants us simply to enjoy them for what they do best, serving satisfying meals and often placing an agreeable stranger on the stool beside us. He hopes that the stranger will enlighten us in some way and become a new friend. It was Randy who generously pointed me down the right paths to the best diners in New England.

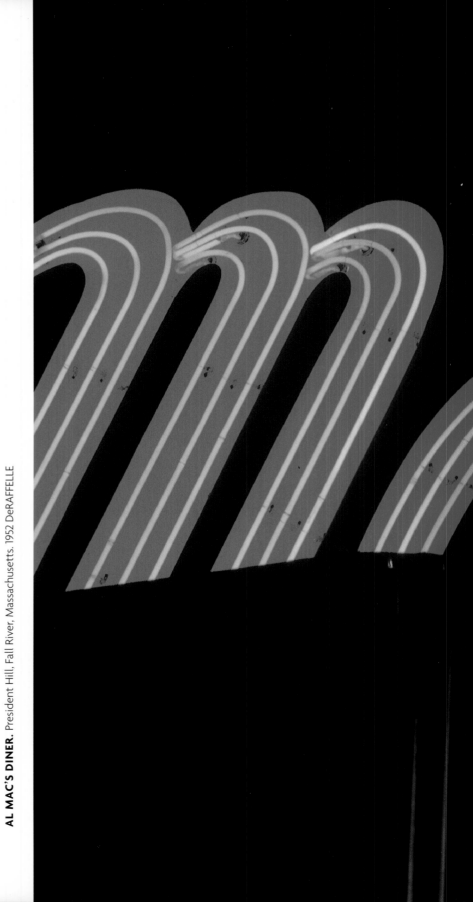

AL MAC'S DINER. President Hill, Fall River, Massachusetts. 1952 DeRAFFELLE

BOULEVARD DINER. Shrewsbury Street, Worcester, Massachusetts. 1936 WORCESTER.

First and foremost, this is a classic piece of well-preserved architecture regarded by many as the finest example of a Worcester diner anywhere. It has appeared in books, paintings, and advertisements. When you step inside you are just as taken back by the grain of the burled oak booths as you are by the aroma of the grille.

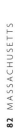

Fittingly, Miss Worcester sits opposite the building where all the Worcester diners were constructed. The factory building still exists, but its doors have been closed for more than thirty years. If you look closely at the building, which is not seen in this photograph, you can still make out the lettering "Worcester Lunch Car Company." And as you daydream in a booth at the Miss Woo you can visualize across the way fifty men working on the skeletons of five diners in various stages of completion.

MISS WORCESTER DINER. Southbridge Street, Worcester, Massachusetts. 1947 WORCESTER.

CASEY'S DINER. South Avenue, Natick, Massachusetts. 1922 WORCESTER.

As far as I can tell, this is the longest continually running family diner that hasn't outgrown its original home. The first time I visited Casey's I didn't know that they closed for most of the month of August. When I saw that closed sign in the window, my heart dropped. Then I saw someone moving around inside the diner, and before I could knock, the side door slid open. There stood Joe Casey, father of the present owner, looking like a New Englander on vacation.

Joe explained that he was just looking in on the diner while it was closed, and he invited me to the annual marathon cleaning the week before fall reopening. While we were talking, his son Fred arrived, a bear of a man with little apparent resemblance to his dad except in his hard work ethic. Joe introduced me and together they showed me around a living museum. The diner truly is a bridge between a lunch wagon and what we think of as a diner. It may only have ten stools, but it does a business greater than many diners ten times its size. Central to the counter is a huge copper kettle, where the hot dog buns are steamed to perfection. No one could come close to figuring out how many dogs

have been sold during the seventy-plus years of operation since Joe's father, also named Fred, started this dynasty. The walls are lined with photos of Natick's bygone days, featuring military parades and historic celebrations of various kinds. The wood ceiling at first looks scorched, but in reality, it is varnish that has bubbled and cracked from the steam inside and the frigid winters outside.

While we were chatting outside several diner regulars passed by, each ready to share the past as if it were yesterday. Fred also shared with me his large collection of books about diners. I hadn't known that there was so much diner history published.

I've been back to Casey's several times, watching a lunch rush where men in suits eagerly await their sandwiches alongside the school kids who frequent this mecca. Sadly, I would never see Joe Casey again; he passed away in 1996. The diner, however, goes on remarkably well with Fred Casey in charge, and his father and grandfather live on in every hot dog that is sold.

CHARLIE'S DINER.
Plantation Street,
Worcester, Massachusetts.
1946 WORCESTER.

I was captivated by Charlie Turner's ad for his diner in *Roadside* magazine: TOUR BUSES WELCOME, it read. You might expect a big establishment, but this is a small, well-run diner that embraces its history but gets on with the business at hand. It creates outstanding food at reasonable prices and serves it up with warmth.

CORNER LUNCH. Lamartine Street, Worcester, Massachusetts. Late 1950's DeRAFFELLE/MUSI

This diner is a Jersey girl in the sea of Worcester Misses. In a town that was home to the Worcester Dining Car Company someone snuck this one in. It is a DeRaffelle diner with a Musi renovation.

Paul Pourier, the quiet young man who owns the Corner Lunch, was the first diner man who welcomed me in to a diner's inner sanctum, its kitchen. The kitchen of a diner tells all. I watched in amazement as Paul whipped up a Friday night menu that had me salivating. I still remember the seafood dinner I ate at the counter. At the same counter sat Paul's mother, Lorraine, who proclaimed that she had taught Paul everything he knows about cooking. I soon realized that she

was not exaggerating: she, too, owns a diner, the Central Diner in Milbury, Massachusetts. Lorraine's diner is an old model Worcester, in which all the cooking is done out front for the customers to watch, and where she manages to bake thirty or more delectable pies each week. Paul also provided me with my first boost of confidence when he hung above the counter my photograph of three elder statesman at his morning breakfast roundtable .

ABOVE: Renee Bombredi collects an order on a busy Friday night.

Renee Bombredi relaxes
between lunch and dinner
in a back booth.

MY TINMAN.
MacArthur Boulevard (the Otis Rotary),
Pocasset, Massachusetts.
1940 DOUBLE-ENDED STERLING STREAMLINER.

My Tinman diner isn't the biggest or shiniest diner, but it's the one whose heart is larger than all the rest, and the reason for that is the owner, Barbara Lind. Any customer who reciprocates the courtesy that Barbara extends automatically becomes a member of the Tinman family. (Anyone who doesn't, gets tossed out.) Barbara's regulars are mostly local, many of them military people from the nearby Otis Air National Guard base. She inspires such loyalty among this clientele that one time, when she had lost her home and was living in the back room of the diner, a couple of local contractors came in and built her a new bathroom in a day.

My Tinman is one of five Sterling Streamliners still functioning. It used to be known as Jimmy Evans Flyer. Its present name is thought by many to be after the Tin Man in *The Wizard of Oz*, but it is actually named for Barbara's grandfather, Charlie Truelson, a scrap dealer, or tin man. Charlie was closer than a father to Barbara, and when he passed away she cried for a week. In sympathy, customers began bringing her posters, dolls, and other memorabilia from *The Wizard of Oz*, and the diner is now crowded with them.

The first time I met Barbara was the week before her first grandchild was due to be born. She insisted that I wait to make my photographs of the diner until her daughter, Susan, arrived. Meanwhile, she told me that this expectant mother had been very ill as a baby and was never supposed to be able to have children, yet here she was, healthy and a week away from delivery. Love and pride beamed forth from her, and the photograph I made of mother and daughter (and granddaughter-to-be) is one of my favorites from the diner road.

I returned to visit Barbara to see two-years' worth of baby pictures of Mesa Mae (born October 4, 1995) and a handful of snapshots of a second grandchild. Not so happy to share were stories of some medical problems, battles with a landlord, and struggles to give up smoking. She also told me that the diner seems to be inhabited by a ghost, but this didn't bother her a bit. Barbara's spirit was undiminished, and I left wishing that My Tinman was closer to my home and that, like the other regulars, I could partake of Barbara's generous caring for the Tinman Family.

OPPOSITE:
Barbara Lind and Susan in front of the diner.

The double-ended Sterling Streamliner is a rare beauty.

The Rosebud has been reborn as an elegant bar and restaurant, a place that provided a welcome haven for me at the end of a whirlwind diner hunting trip.

ROSEBUD DINER. Summer Street, Somerville, Massachusetts. 1940's WORCESTER.

The Central is so old that it has no inside bathroom (not required in 1933), and the dishwashing takes place in tubs next to the counter. These inconveniences scarcely bother owner Lorraine Augusto, a dynamo who bakes some thirty pies each week and serves home-cooked food that rivals gourmet restaurants.

CENTRAL DINER. Elm Street, Milbury, Massachusetts. 1933 WORCESTER.

NITE OWL DINER.
Pleasant Street,
Fall River, Massachusetts.
1956 DeRAFFELLE.

The Nite Owl is a contradiction in terms, because it is only open from six o'clock in the morning to two o'clock in the afternoon, with no nite hours whatever. Instead, the Nite Owl perches on its triangular corner and is lighted for most of its day by sun streaming through big pane windows. The place might have been better named the Comedy Club, however, because the regulars who come for breakfast are a real bunch of wits. If you're in the diner when one of the group is approaching, the comedians inside will regale you with that person's life story in hilarious detail.

You are also apt to see just as much food carried into the diner as is sold within. It doesn't seem to bother the owner a bit that the regulars bring in their ethnic delicacies, often sharing them with newcomers like me. This place may be small in size, but it's big in warmth.

OPPOSITE:
An old soul watches the world go by from the Nite Owl.

Breakfast at the counter window.

Phil Paleologis poses on the roof of his cherished diner.

SHAWMUT DINER.

Shawmut Avenue,
New Bedford, Massachusetts.
1957 O'MAHONY

The Shawmut might better rename itself the Welcome Diner. Its owner, Phil Paleologis, and his family make every customer a friend. The first time I journeyed to the Shawmut I was out front snapping pictures when the hostess came out and chastised me for not saying hello. I felt self-conscious telling her that I was a journalist from Philadelphia documenting diner culture in America. I thought she was going to tell me to pack it up unless I had the owner's permission to take pictures. Instead, she said that when I was done taking my photos I should come inside for breakfast—on the house, courtesy of the owner. I've been back again and again, not just for a free meal.

If you hear Phil Paleologis speak you'll understand why he doubles as a radio talk show host. Phil used to commute to a distant radio studio to do his show, but he has simplified life by removing a back booth in the diner and installing a state of the art broadcast setup. As he discusses lively national issues with callers-in he also draws on the opinions of his audience of early risers at the diner.

A McDonald's restaurant opened up diagonally across the street from the Shawmut, but if anything it increased business rather than taking it away. Quality speaks.

EDGEMERE DINER. Hartford Pike, Shrewsbury, Massachusetts. 1940 FODERO.

I'm surprised that the clock in the Edgemere Diner in Shrewsbury, Massachusetts, is still there, considering all the offers to buy it. Almost any art museum would be proud to display this Fodero clock, very few of which still exist.

Mayvette Burt, age 4 at this time, and the daughter of the owner of the Edgemere, looks a little apprehensive as a busload of diner lovers point their cameras her way.

FILL'IN STATION DINER. Route 5 off Interstate 91, Whately, Massachusetts. 1960 KULLMAN.

The name says it all at this diner along the Interstate just south of the Vermont border, a fueling and rest stop for big tractor trailers. Like the rigs outside, which never turn the engines off, the place has a nervous hum. The customers inside are a mix of truckers and local kids in the back booths drinking coffee.

The famous old east-west highway, Route 66, can't be found within 1,000 miles of this diner, but owner Don Roy clearly had a soft spot for the name.

ROUTE 66 DINER. Bay Street, Springfield, Massachusetts. 1957 MOUNTAIN VIEW.

Appropriately in the town notorious for colonial era witch hunts, my visit to the Salem Diner was on Halloween in 1994, and a good witch served me an incredible crabcake dinner. This Sterling Streamliner has incredible glass counter tops, in which the owners used to place pies directly under the unsuspecting customers' noses. What advertising savvy to create such temptations.

SALEM DINER. Canal Street, Salem, Massachusetts. 1941 STERLING STREAMLINER.

MORAN SQUARE DINER. Myrtle Avenue, Fitchburg, Massachusetts. 1940 WORCESTER.

You cannot make a bad photograph of this diner, which sits proudly on the town square, where it has no doubt been the best seat for fifty years of July Fourth parades. In the fall of 1994 I met the new owners, Chris and Mary Gianetti, who were working hard to create a new menu to follow that of the former owner, Louis Vitelli.

Chris has a degree from Johnson and Wales Culinary College, and Mary is a certified dietician, so their intention has been to create a menu with healthy choices and something less than mammoth propor-

tions. But each time they vary the formula, regular patrons complain that Louis would never serve it that way. They have realized that they bought more than a building on Moran Square; they bought a tradition, and changing it will be slow work, but with a delicious future.

OPPOSITE:
A satisfied customer of the Moran Square Diner.

CAPITOL DINER. Union Street, Lynn, Massachusetts. 1920s BRILL.

The Capitol sits sideways on a small lot in Lynn, where a fenced-in area corrals a goat and a flock of chickens—the only petting zoo in the city. The seventy-year-old diner has been owned by the Fennell family for fifty years; Buddy Fennell still works there every day, but son Bobby often takes over the grill despite also serving as a state representative from Lynn. Bobby always appears in a starched white shirt and colorful tie with never a hair out of place, and invariably wearing a broad smile. Before entering the diner on any given day, Bobby has shaken twenty hands and listened to the concerns of forty voters. The diner acts as a de facto political arena for his constituency, and between good food, good advice, and a sympathetic ear, everyone is well served.

FOUR SISTERS OWL DINER.

Appleton Street, Lowell, Massachusetts.
1940 WORCESTER

You don't find the best waitress, she finds you. She's a tornado blowing through a diner, a manifestation of pure energy, with a personality so real that you may think it's an act. She calls the customers she has met before by name and those she meets for the first time "Hon." By the end of a first visit she'll know a customer's name, where they are from, and how many kids they have. She never lets a coffee cup lie empty, she doesn't need to write an order down even if there are substitutions, and she'll brighten the day better than any tonic could.

With due respect to all the amazing waitresses I have met, my personal pick for number one goes to Martha Quinn of the Four Sisters Owl Diner. Martha may have reached mid-life, but her energy rivals that of any 16-year-old. She buzzes through the diner filling ketchup bottles, taking orders, and delivering others. You'd swear she was using magic, she's so fast. I've heard that one afternoon she put on roller skates and performed her entire shift without dropping a plate. But other diner waitresses are fast. What sets Martha apart is that she is always laughing or giggling, nonstop. She'll sit down in the empty spot in your booth like your best friend from high school and help you catch up on your own life.

Martha is one of four sisters, all of them skilled waitresses, and one of them a co-owner of the diner with her husband. Yet one sister told me that when Martha first set foot in the diner she had never waited a table in her life. She was shy and quiet, hiding in the back until her orders were ready to be delivered. Little by little, however, the atmosphere of the diner drew her out and she became a world-class waitress. If you're lucky and arrive at the diner on a particular day all four sisters will be working the counter.

Mary Beth and Martha, two of the four sisters.

MISS ADAMS DINER.

Park Street, Adams, Massachusetts.
1949 WORCESTER.

Considered by experts as the best-run diner in America with the most original menu, the Miss Adams Diner stands in Massachusetts but has the feel of Vermont (it's only seven miles from the border). If you're puzzled by a sign that reads "DRINK SQUEEZE," you'll soon learn that Miss Adams serves neither Coke nor Pepsi but Squeeze, a beverage produced right up the road in Adams. This sets the tone for the diner, which seems to march to its own drummer. Barry and Nancy Garton, who run the diner, complement one another well. Barry, the chef, creates a menu so tempting that I never eat just one entree; Nancy knows every customer and their favorite dishes. Those who travel are so loyal that they confess to Nancy if they have eaten in another diner while they were away, always adding that "it wasn't nearly as good as the food here." Barry can't relax, even a little. Very little leaves the kitchen that doesn't bear his distinct mark. The glass display rack out front is full of fresh hot muffins in as many as six varieties. Never ask him for something he doesn't have, because he'll get it for you. And never be afraid to try what seem like exotic entrees at the Miss Adams; you'll get a new taste treat.

Nancy Garton tops off a customer's coffee.

MAINE

MISS BRUNSWICK DINER.
Pleasant Street,
Brunswick, Maine.
1938 WORCESTER.

Henry Thiboutot, age 62, has
been a customer of the Miss
Brunswick since 1948. It was here
that he courted his wife, who
now works as a waitress at the
diner. Not much of the original
diner exists, but the customers
look as if they have been loyal
since childhood.

OPPOSITE:
MISS PORTLAND DINER.
Marginal Way,
Portland, Maine.
1949 WORCESTER.

The Worcester clock and stainless steel backsplash in the
well-preserved Miss Portland
Diner in Portland, Maine.

A-1 DINER.
Bridge Street, Gardiner, Maine.
1946 WORCESTER.

I've seen diners as far away from my home outside Philadelphia as Florida and California, but I've never driven any farther just to see a diner than I did to see the A-1. If you know Maine then you know that there's a lot of it, followed by a lot more of it. Gardiner is well past Portland, between Augusta and the coast. When I journeyed there it was on a marathon driving tour that had started twenty hours earlier, and was punctuated by visits to diners along the way. Not a smart move on my part; I was exhausted. What's more, mid-coast Maine had just experienced the worst ice storm in forty years and was still reeling from its effects. As I drove along the Kennebec River I saw thousands of trees that had been snapped off like toothpicks four feet above the ground. When I finally got to Gardiner at 8:30 P.M. I found a motel with a vacancy and fell asleep as soon as my head touched the pillow.

After a 6 A.M. wake-up call I headed straight over to the A-1. As I had been told, this very pretty diner sits on stilts alongside a bridge into town. You can walk down a set of steps and look under the diner. I did so, and got a huge fright as forty pigeons that I had disturbed flew past my head.

I discovered that the diner didn't open until 7 A.M., and the air was painfully cold. I was unprepared, having come the day before from Philadelphia, where temperatures were in the sixties. So I sat in my Explorer until the doors opened. At 7 A.M. on the dot, I stepped into the A-1, and felt immediately warm. To my surprise, the place was already nearly full, and I quickly learned that the diner regulars sneak in through the kitchen door before the place opens. Tony Bennett was playing on the stereo and the smell of fresh coffee permeated the air. I felt right at home.

James Whalen, age 70, a lifetime local resident and A-1 patron.

The original name of the diner, Heald's, still is etched on the porcelain panels. Daylight on this day was dulled by clouds rich with snow flurries. One of the owners, Neal Anderson, relaxes out front.

PALACE DINER.
Westland Avenue, Biddeford, Maine.
1920s POLLARD.

I visited the Palace Diner, the only
known Pollard diner in existence, on
my way back home after a trip Down
East. I planned on staying only for
coffee, but remained for three hours,
ate the largest lunch of my life, and
felt like I met the entire town of
Biddeford. Rich Bernier, owner of the
diner, came home one day in 1997
and told his wife that he had bought
himself a new job, a diner. Bernier
smiles like a man who knows a secret.
Well, it's not a secret any more, since
everyone knows that this is the best
meal in town. I suggested to Rich that
he could cut back on his portions by
25 percent, since most people can't
finish their meals. He smiled, thanked
me for the compliment, and added
an extra piece of turkey to my plate.

Rich Bernier in traditional dress
whites.

NEW HAMPSHIRE

The Tumble Inn forms a link in a small chain of diners whose base is at Ken Smith's Daddypop's Diner in Hatboro, Pennsylvania. Ken's daughter, Debbie, and son-in-law Paul Carter own the place but it bears Ken's quirky mark.

John Baeder's painting of the Tumble Inn was always one of my favorites, and I felt like I was entering the painting when I opened the door the first time. Then I got a shock, however, for the diner had literally been pulled apart to repair years of neglect. The place looked like the pieces of a disassembled clock, every piece present but a seemingly impossible task to put back together. Paul Carter was working night and day stripping layers of paint from the delicate wooden trim and laminate ceiling panels. He smiled and assured me that he would be operational by the month's end. I smiled back, even though my head was throbbing from the idea of his gargantuan task. I made a few pictures of the exterior and vowed to return when the place was open.

I heard through the grapevine that the Tumble Inn opened two months later and was doing well. Truly the Doubting Thomas, I had to see for myself, but nearly a year and a half passed by the time I could return. Debbie and Paul had not only put the pieces back together again in the right order but they had also stamped the diner with a true personality, not unlike that of the Daddypop's.

The diner gleamed from every surface, red gingham curtains hung from every window, and every booth was filled with customers. Though busy, Paul greeted me with a vigorous, warm handshake, apologizing for his wet hands. He introduced me to Debbie, who may not look exactly like her dad but is the mirror of his personality. I watched Debbie and Paul work together in the close confines of the grill, which is out front for all to see: this is like performing a play in the nude. But the couple love each other and love their diner. They really feel blessed, and, despite the long hours, are helping to revitalize the town of Claremont through every meal they serve at the Tumble Inn.

OPPOSITE:
Debbie Carter lends a shoulder
to her daughter, Fallon.

TUMBLE INN DINER. Main Street, Claremont, New Hampshire. 1940 WORCESTER.

A shy little customer wriggles and squirms during breakfast at the Tumble Inn.

This Worcester diner has a two-story frame building completely enveloping it. In architectural terms, this is a diner travesty, but open the door and the Four Aces reveals a perfect fifties interior.

The Four Aces was one of those places where the customers were eager to share their memories with me. One man went so far as to insist that I follow him down the road to see the longest covered bridge in New England. Though not a big covered bridge fan, I was taken by the man's enthusiasm and his willingness to direct a perfect stranger to a piece of local history. We could all take a lesson from this: be proud of the landmarks in our communities and share them with strangers.

FOUR ACES DINER. Bridge Street, West Lebanon, New Hampshire. 1950s WORCESTER.

The two women in the photo were very shy about having their picture taken. They talked with me extensively, but wouldn't let me take more than the one that you see. They wanted to know all about my diner project, how far I'd traveled, and which diners were my favorites. I learned that one of the women had raised her family in Drexel Hill, Pennsylvania, which is next to Havertown, where I lived for several years. I was entranced by these ladies and quite sad to be able to make only one photograph, but I was rewarded when the film came back.

GLORY JEANS DINER. Route 25, Rumney, New Hampshire. 1954 O'MAHONY.

I was looking for this diner in the middle of a long road to nowhere and to make sure I hadn't passed it I stopped at a gas station. Inside I was greeted by a living Norman Rockwell painting: four men in plaid wool hunting coats and flap-eared hats warming themselves around a pot-belly stove. They let me know in as few words as possible that I still had a few miles to go. (I've found more than once that I have a few more miles to go.)

VERMONT

PARKWAY DINER.
Williston Road,
South Burlington, Vermont.
1950s WORCESTER.

This magnificent diner was produced during the last days of the Worcester Dining Car Company. When I went to find it, first thing on a Monday morning, I had the privilege of meeting Peter Hatgen, the proud Greek man who owns the diner, and George Alvanos, who now cooks and runs it day to day. Peter and I talked about many things, especially the beauty of his homeland, and he showed me in the diner a stained glass rendering of the fishing village that was his boyhood home. When we wandered back to the subject of the diner that he loves, Peter told me that at seventy-five he had chosen to enjoy life more, and that he had entrusted the diner to George (shown here at the grill).

OPPOSITE:
YANKEE DINER.
Route 4, Quechee, Vermont.
1946 WORCESTER.

When I last visited this diner, which was formerly called the Ross Diner, it was destined to change its name for the third time, becoming the Farina Family Diner. This photograph still shows the Yankee logo reflected in the snow puddle out front, where I stood with my boots leaking at 6 A.M. to make this sunrise shot. I literally watched the sun rise over the mountain and shine down into Quechee Gorge. A few minutes later, as I sat twisting the ice water from my socks, I was greeted by Ron Farina, the new owner, along with his sons, Chris and Jay. Ron thought that he would never leave Rhode Island, but when some of his family moved to Vermont he became convinced to set up camp here with his sons. If enthusiasm counts for anything, the Farina Family will have already made this diner a winner by the time these photographs appear.

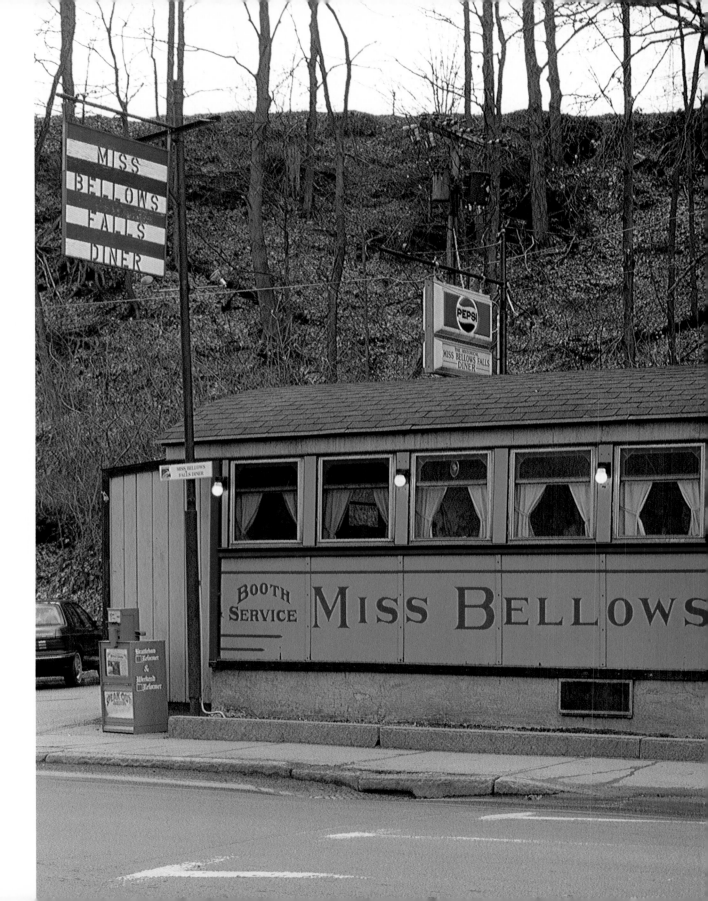

MISS BELLOWS FALLS DINER.

Rockingham Street,
Bellows Falls, Vermont.
1940 WORCESTER.

I first visited Miss Bellows Falls, one of seven diners currently on the National Historic Register, in the fall of 1996. The sun never shined for four straight days, but I returned with my guides, Randy Garbin and Susan Germain, two years later during an unseasonably warm weekend at the end of winter.

BIRDSEYE DINER. Main Street, Castleton, Vermont. 1949 SILK CITY.

This diner, which had been covered in barn siding, was a hidden treasure until 1995, when restorationist Daniel Zilka performed his magic by putting new porcelain panels on it. The interior of the Birdseye illustrates the detailed craftsmanship characteristic of Silk City diners: superb prefabricated architecture.

MIDWAY DINER.
Route 22A, Ordwell, Vermont.
1951 SILK CITY.

This beauty truly seems midway, between one life and another. I was on my way to Burlington, Vermont, when I spotted this glowing gem in a farmyard. I slammed on my brakes and waded through a foot of spring mud to set up my tripod. Most diners look pathetic as they sit abandoned or closed, but the Midway, formerly of Rutland, Vermont, still had a certain regal quality. With any luck, it will be back in operation soon.

NEW YORK

New York City is not exactly what we think of as a hometown. It's an international place, home to the United Nations, headquarters of hundreds of multinational corporations, and filled with tourists and immigrants from every corner of the planet. As a result, hometown-style diner hunting in New York is difficult. New York has hundreds of restaurants that call themselves diners, but in reality perhaps only a dozen traditional diners exist in Manhattan.

The reasons are fairly simple: real estate in Manhattan is among the priciest in the world. Traditional diners are one-story structures and very few pieces of land in Manhattan can be afforded for anything less than a ten-story building. Forty years ago diners thrived because odd parcels of land still existed. Today diners are in a distinct minority, competing with coffee shops tucked into the ground floors of office buildings on virtually every corner.

The River Diner across from the Javits Center, and the Munson at the corner of Eleventh Avenue and Forty-ninth Street are largely supported by taxi drivers. The River Diner is located next to a taxi garage, and mechanics and drivers flow back and forth between the two places. The adventuresome conventioneer at the Javits Center may occasionally dodge traffic to experience this New York institution.

The Cheyenne Diner on Ninth Avenue near Madison Square Garden doesn't just wait for customers; the management fields a diligent patrol of bike soldiers who deliver take-out food to office buildings in the area. The Cheyenne has served as a backdrop to dozens of photographic spreads by the town's premier fashion magazines. The owner proudly posts tearsheets of the stories shot in his diner.

The Empire Diner, despite being criticized as an upscale restaurant hiding in the clothes of a humble diner, nevertheless is the focal point of its neighborhood. The park across the way often fills with young parents pushing their children on the swings as old men play chess under the trees. Before sitting down to eat at the Empire I recommend taking a walk around the block. Some of the finest homes in Manhattan grace

RIVER DINER. Eleventh Avenue, Manhattan. Late 1930s KULLMAN.

the surrounding streets. Look up at the facades, admire the wrought iron fences, smell the flowers in window-box planters. If time and weather permit, sit at a table in front of the diner and watch New York pass by.

The other few classic diners in Manhattan are rather melancholy. Their beauty has been compromised by neglect or thoughtless renovation. Their days are numbered. But New York is more than Manhattan, and among the other boroughs—the Bronx, Brooklyn, Queens, and Staten Island—are distinct communities with neighborhoods, and among those neighborhoods are diners.

Queens, for example, is rich in diners and I took a whirlwind tour of them with the local tracker and guide, Mario Monti, a retired schoolteacher who calls Forest Hills home. There are more than sixty diners in

Queens, although half of them are closed or on hard times. Mario and his enthusiasm propelled me along as we visited lively places like the Deerhead on Astoria Boulevard, a one-of-a-kind Paramount from the early 1960s. It is a bridge between classic stainless diners and the enormous stone-facaded restaurants that have dominated since the late 1960s. There we met Margie Clark, a waitress who was friendly, but cautious about these two strangers who were asking far too many questions about the diner. Sipping our coffee, we gazed out the huge pane windows, where only a week before another classic diner, the Buccaneer, had stood. All that remained was the sign and a pile of rubble.

But there are other diners out there, and Mario Monti intends to find them all. I await my next phone call from him with great enthusiasm.

CHEYENNE DINER. Ninth Avenue, Manhattan. 1946 PARAMOUNT.

A rainy night in the Big Apple.

MUNSON DINER.
Eleventh Avenue, Manhattan.
1946 KULLMAN.

New York City's taxi drivers
know where to park and eat
good and cheap at any time
of day or night. Follow the
Yellow cab.

EMPIRE DINER. Tenth Avenue, Manhattan. 1946 FODERO

A corner window at the
Empire Diner is a window on
the whole world.

MOONDANCE DINER.
Avenue of the Americas at Grand Street, Manhattan. Diner maker and date unknown.

A glitzy sign distinguishes an otherwise dull diner facade.

JACKSON HOLE, WYOMING.
Astoria Boulevard,
Queens, New York.
1950s MOUNTAIN VIEW.

The remaining original
neon sign of the Air Line
Diner belies the fact that
it has been taken over by
the Jackson Hole Wyoming
chain of restaurants.

DEERHEAD DINER. Astoria Boulevard, Queens, New York. Early 1960s PARAMOUNT.

RIVERHEAD GRILL.
East Main Street, Riverhead, Long Island.
1940s KULLMAN.

Owner Liz Strebel has the best smile in the diner business, and exudes class as she works the grill, which is still out front. She has a loyal following of breakfast club old-timers who are all, not surprisingly, secretly in love with her.

Mario Monti, who looks
and seems far younger
than his sixty-eight years,
has made it his task to
document the more than
eighty-five diners of
Queens. Many are tucked
away in places so out of
the way that even Mario
must consult a map to
find them. We met at the
Deerhead Diner, located
near LaGuardia Airport,
which hosts a cast of
characters who seem as if
they've just answered a
call for a Scorcese movie.

Margie Clark has the look of experience from her years of tenure as a waitress at the Deerhead Diner.

GIBBY'S DINER.
Route 7, Quakerstreet, New York.
1953 MOUNTAIN VIEW.

This is a little diner, with sparkling additions on both ends and flower boxes at every window. It looks as though the owners loved their diner so much that they cut their house down the middle and put a diner inside.

I usually sneak into a diner and try to be as unobtrusive as possible, but my memory of Gibby's was shared with about five dozen other diner enthusiasts because I first visited it as a participant of the Diner Convention in 1997.

The homestyle breakfast we were served was truly incredible. About midway through the meal a charming man in a white shirt introduced himself as Gibby and proceeded to tell us the history of his diner. Gibby loved his diner and told us that he had recently semi-retired, but his whole speech was punctuated with the sense that he considered each customer as family. I don't think there was a dry eye in the house when he finished, including mine, and I'm a pretty unsentimental sort. Sixty people got their cameras out and Gibby obliged by posing for each one of them. I've never met a diner owner who gave more of a sense of why diners are so special, nor heard more pride from any diner owner about why he spent his life feeding others.

MISS ALBANY DINER. Broadway, Albany, New York. 1941 SILK CITY.

This diner was reborn during the filming of *Ironweed*, a movie about the Great Depression starring Jack Nicholson and Meryl Streep. The film takes place in a time before this diner was even built, but never mind.

Cliff Brown, the owner of Miss Albany, is an inveterate tinkerer. He redug the basement of the diner when he needed to expand the floor space above, and installed a dumbwaiter to connect the two areas when there wasn't room to put in a proper staircase. Cliff gives his customers a choice of French fries in three degrees of crispness. His wife just smiles. Once a month he closes the diner on Friday night and serves a seven-course gourmet dinner to those who are fortunate enough to get on his list, which means applying months in advance. For most of the world just eating his fish fry on an ordinary Friday is heaven enough. The neighborhood around the Miss Albany Diner needs a boost, and Cliff Brown does his best to provide it.

DOC'S LITTLE GEM DINER.
Spencer Street, Syracuse, New York.
1957 FODERO.

Before I ever considered diners more than a place for a good meal, I used to nurse a hangover in the booths of the Little Gem. I was a student at Syracuse University at the time, majoring in Party 101. The Little Gem was neither the shiniest nor the best diner in Syracuse, but it never closed. This was critical for anyone cranking out a term paper at two o'clock in the morning. We shouldn't regret what might have been, but I regret that I never thought to raise my camera even once on all those trips to the Little Gem. The things we take for granted in life are often those that are most cherished later on. The Little Gem stands high on my personal list for preservation.

OPPOSITE:
Doc's Little Gem sees the sun rise on Good Friday morning, 1996.

HIGHLAND PARK DINER. South Clinton Street, Rochester, New York. 1948 ORLEANS.

It was almost two years into my project before I saw the most beautiful diner in America. The diner listing I consulted showed that the Highland Park was designated as having been constructed on site, usually the kiss of death for diner architecture. In reality the Highland Park's builders, Orleans Diners, put the parts together on site but in every sense they fabricated a classic diner. The documentation on how many Orleans Diners were built is sketchy, probably three, but the Highland Park is the only survivor. It is also the only original diner in Rochester, which used to be a real diner town, supporting more than ten.

The original name of the diner was Danphin's Superior Diner, and it was run by Ed and Ann Danphin until 1974. It had a humiliating second life as an Off Track Betting parlor from 1976 to 1986, but then it found Bob Malley. Malley is a perfectionist. He owned Rochester's premier donut shop, Donuts Delite, and he saw the carcass of the Highland Park as the ideal outlet for his donuts. He painstakingly restored the diner to its original glory from photographs and blueprints. When he reopened as a donut shop with a small breakfast menu he was immediately inundated with customer requests for a full range of diner food. Malley has since removed the pastry case and created one of the most original menus in all the diner world.

I'm not really qualified as a food critic, but I believe the Highland Park has the best pie in America. (Their apple pie was cited as the best in America by Conde Nast's *Traveler* magazine.) The pecan pie is my favorite. As for other food, the mashed potatoes are out of this world, not made from flakes but peeled fresh and boiled, just like mom's, and whipped with butter and cream. The Highland Park cooks use a pint of honey for each cooked ham and when they make turkey they cook the whole bird. They spare no expense to provide their customers with food that surpasses most restaurants in every way except perhaps for the size of the check. The waitresses wear period black uniforms that at first glance seem like showmanship, but we shouldn't confuse professionalism with theatrics. Bob Malley and his family run the classiest diner in America. If you're on a quest looking at diners, maybe you should wait a while to visit the Highland Park: save the best for last.

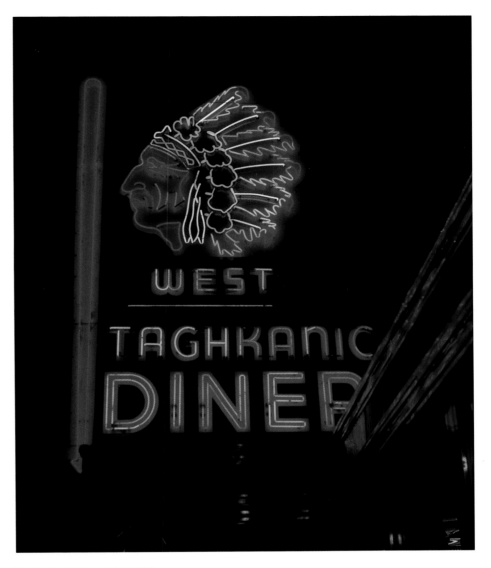

WEST TAGHKANIC DINER.
Route 82 and Taghkanic Parkway,
West Taghkanic, New York.
1953 MOUNTAIN VIEW.

My opinion that this is the finest diner neon is shared by many. The double-sided Indian chief's head gives Las Vegas neon art a run for its money.

EMPIRE DINER.
West Albany Street, Herkimer, New York.
1950 MOUNTAIN VIEW.

This is the only photograph in this book that was planned—a picture of my father with his grandson, Gregory, in the diner of my boyhood. No photo exists of my dad and me at the diner, and I thought it would be only fitting that I take one of my dad with his favorite person in the world, my son Gregory.

My dad and I used to sneak off from our home in the small town of Ilion, New York, to the Empire Diner in Herkimer on Saturday mornings so my mom could sleep late. We'd sit at the counter and have pancakes and maple syrup. My mother was a great cook, but she could never make pancakes like a diner could. (Neither my father nor I ever had the heart to tell her that her pancakes were kind of hard and chewy.) In the diner I would breathe in the air, a mix of cigarettes and black coffee, and listen to the clank of silverware and dishes as Sinatra played on the wall box. For those two hours I was a little man, out with my dad. No memory from my past stirs me as strongly.

My father, a very reserved man, becomes a different person around his grandson; smiling, running, and telling stories of his youth. It took him a long time to understand why I would want to produce a book about diners, let alone make him a part of it. I finally convinced him to take that drive to the Empire Diner. The diner looks much as it did when I was a boy, only it has moved a block away from where it originally stood: it seems that in the early 1970s the owners couldn't resist the offer Burger King made them for the land. The diner sat in storage for about six years until another business on a popular corner in Herkimer burned down. The diner has been reborn on this sunny spot across from the taxi stop.

On my sentimental return to the Empire with my father and Gregory, they sat at the counter eating dessert together while I prowled around looking for the best way to make the photograph. Between my son's fidgeting and my father's self-conscious awareness that others were watching this photo session I thought I'd never get my picture. So I walked away for a while, went to the bathroom, and on returning, I saw the father and the little man from 1963 as you see them here. I had my closing picture.

P.S. I was determined to make this photograph in monochrome: my past seems to play back not in color but in black and white. The quest for the image also taught me an important lesson, that the best pictures are spontaneous. My most successful photographs for this book have appeared before me, only lasting as long as the click of the shutter.

INDEX

ACKNOWLEDGMENTS

This project began in earnest in 1994 as a logical side-line to my other love, photographing classic movie theaters. Because of the living souls of the people who run diners and the regular customers, I found diners easier to translate onto film.

This book would not have been more than wishful thinking without the passionate support, advice, and understanding of Randy Garbin and Susan Germain of *Roadside* magazine. *Roadside* devotes itself to the road less traveled in America.

I would also like here to recognize those spiritual leaders of the diner world, John Baeder and Richard Gutman. John Baeder's book, *Diners*, enticed me to step inside his paintings and meet the people who are at its heart. Richard Gutman, diner historian without equal, wrote a book that offers a rich panorama of the history—the rise, fall, and rebirth—of diners that created a road map for the start my journey.

The journey toward completing this book was smoothed by favor after favor from friends old and new. Special thanks are due: to Melinda Williams for constantly challenging me to push forward on this project; to Ara Nuyujukian at Eastman Kodak, who started his career hawking cameras with me in Philly and provided invaluable technical support on the project; Lisa Barnes of the Berman Museum for taking a chance on my first exhibit of diner photographs; and, lastly, the editing and moral support provided by the suburban photo staff of the *Philadelphia Inquirer*, the greatest group of unsung photographers at any paper in America.

Thanks also to Lori Gitterman, Joseph Homsher, Heinz USA, Larry Kesterson, Kullman Industries, William Linaberry, Mario Monti, Robert Morton, Susan Oyama, Ellen Nygaard, John Shepherd, Sherman Williams, Jonathan Wilson—and all the diner owners and staff I've had the honor to share coffee with.